0 00 30 0325674 4

Albert
Einstein

Other titles in the Inventors and Creators series include:

Alexander Graham Bell
Walt Disney
Thomas Edison
Henry Ford
Benjamin Franklin
Jim Henson
J.K. Rowling
Jonas Salk
Dr. Seuss
Steven Spielberg
The Wright Brothers

Albert
Einstein

Sheila Wyborny

KIDHAVEN
PRESS™

THOMSON
━━━━━━━━━★━━━━━━━━━ ™
GALE

San Diego • Detroit • New York • San Francisco • Cleveland
New Haven, Conn. • Waterville, Maine • London • Munich

© 2003 by KidHaven Press. KidHaven Press is an imprint of The Gale Group, Inc., a division of Thomson Learning, Inc.

KidHaven™ and Thomson Learning™ are trademarks used herein under license.

For more information, contact
KidHaven Press
27500 Drake Rd.
Farmington Hills, MI 48331-3535
Or you can visit our Internet site at http://www.gale.com

LIBRARY OF CONGRESS CATALOGING-IN-PUBLICATION DATA

Wyborny, Sheila, 1950–
  Albert Einstein / by Sheila Wyborny.
    p. cm.—(Inventors and creators)
Summary: A biography of the physicist whose theories of relativity revolutionized the way we look at space and time.
Includes bibliographical references and index.
  ISBN 0-7377-1278-3 (alk. paper)
1. Einstein, Albert, 1879–1955—Juvenile literature. 2. Physicists—Biography—
—Juvenile literature. [1. Einstein, Albert, 1879–1955. 2. Physicists.] I. Title.
II. Series.
  QC16 .E5 W89 2003
  530' .092—dc21

2002004877

AGI -4781

Contents

An Unlikely Hero

Albert Einstein has been called one of the greatest minds in science, but his beginnings were anything but noteworthy. He hardly spoke until he was three years old, showed violent fits of temper as a child, and was a loner. In school he studied only what interested him and interrupted classes by endlessly questioning his teachers. As a teenager he had a reputation among his teachers of being disrespectful and sarcastic. And in college he skipped many of his classes because the subject matter bored him.

As a young adult, Einstein scrambled for jobs to support himself. He also had to face his shortcomings. He had serious problems with authority, both with his teachers and with some of his early employers. To be successful he had to change the way he dealt with people in authority.

When he finally found full-time work, he was a competent and thorough worker. He also spent a lot of time studying the subjects that most interested him:

Albert Einstein, physicist and creator of important scientific theories.

mathematics and science. And because of his studies, he came up with many important scientific **theories**.

After a slow start, Einstein's theories spread among scientists throughout the world. Many people began to recognize him as a genius and he became a respected teacher, researcher, and guest lecturer. Einstein's work and ideas also led to many important inventions including television, the laser, and the atomic bomb. And because he was so influential, his work is still studied by new generations of scientists around the world.

Chapter One

Differences and Difficulties

On March 14, 1879, a baby boy was born to a young Jewish couple in Ulm, Germany. The new parents named the baby Albert. Little did Hermann and Pauline Einstein know that their firstborn would grow up to be one of the world's most famous scientists.

Little Albert

At first, Albert's mother and grandmother were worried about the new baby. His grandmother thought he was too heavy. "Much too fat! Much too fat!"[1] she said. And his mother worried because his head was large. She feared that he might be slightly retarded.

As time passed, the Einsteins noticed something else different about Albert. As a toddler, Albert did not talk. If fact, until he was three years old he spoke very little. One exception was when his sister Maja was born. Albert was two at the time and asked his parents where her wheels were. The young boy thought a baby sister was a type of toy, and most of his toys had wheels. It did not matter what he said, though. His parents were happy to hear Albert say anything.

Einstein (right) and his sister, Maja, hold hands in a picture that was taken around 1888.

Childhood Conflicts

By the time Maja was born, the family had moved to Munich, Germany. There, Hermann Einstein, an engineer, went into business building electronic equipment with his brother, Jakob.

The elder Einsteins had a great influence on Albert and Maja. Through their father and their Uncle Jakob, also an engineer, the Einstein children were exposed to mathematics. Their mother, a talented pianist, surrounded them with music. Albert briefly took violin lessons, but one day in a fit of temper, he hit his teacher with his violin. This ended his lessons.

Albert had other problems with his temper. When he became angry, he often threw or broke things. Once, he even hit his sister Maja with a garden hoe.

Einstein learned to play the violin as a child. Later in life he played the instrument for his own enjoyment.

But when he finally learned to control his temper, Albert and his sister became good friends and playmates.

Curiosity

When Albert was five, he became ill and had to spend a few days in bed. To help pass the time, his father gave him a compass as a toy. Albert was very interested in how the needle of the compass moved. No matter which way Albert faced, the needle on the compass always pointed in the same direction. This aroused Albert's curiosity; and he wanted to understand how the compass worked.

Albert received another present that peaked his curiosity: a model steam engine. His uncle, Caesar Koch, his mother's brother, gave him this toy. Albert liked to examine the model engine run to understand how it worked.

Albert also enjoyed building with blocks and making houses with playing cards. He was careful and patient while building his playing card houses. He once built a card house that was fourteen stories high, a very difficult accomplishment.

Although he liked these games and toys, Albert rarely played with other children. He preferred to keep to himself. This continued as he started school.

Growing Up Different

As a young student, Albert worked hard and made good grades. From the beginning he was especially good at mathematics. But he did not like school very much and did not mix with the other boys. They were interested in playing sports and pretending they were soldiers. Albert, though, preferred reading and studying to play.

The older Albert became, the less he liked school. He did not like to sit still and memorize lessons. And he asked so many questions in class that some of his teachers thought he was stupid. During the generation when Albert Einstein was in school, students were expected to sit quietly and memorize their lessons. They did not raise their hands and question their teachers.

Albert did pay attention to subjects that interested him, however. When he was twelve, a family friend, Max Talmud, gave him a geometry book. Albert quickly mastered all of the problems in the book. Later, Talmud gave Albert a science book about stars, gravity, atoms, and electricity. Albert was very interested in this as well. He also studied an algebra book his Uncle Jakob gave him. Soon Albert was spending most of his time studying math and science, giving little attention to his other subjects.

Trouble at School

In 1888 Albert began classes at the Luitpold Gymnasium. This school had a very strict environment. Teachers loudly scolded students who did not do their homework or did not perform well in class. Once Albert made a poor grade in his Greek class. Instead of trying to help Albert improve his grade, the teacher told him he would never amount to anything. This made Albert dislike school even more.

When Albert was fifteen, his father's business in Germany failed and the family had to move to Milan,

A painting from 1950 shows Einstein writing out scientific equations.

Italy, where his father and his uncle felt business opportunities would be better. Albert stayed behind in Germany, living in a boardinghouse so he could finish school.

Albert was miserable with this arrangement, though, and he had an idea he thought would solve his problems. He talked his family's doctor into writing a letter to the school. The letter explained how upset Albert was over the absence of his family, and it excused him from classes so he could go see his family.

Little did Albert know that the note was unnecessary. Before he could take the note to the principal, he was kicked out of school because his teachers thought he was disrespectful and inattentive.

A New Land for Albert

At fifteen, Albert traveled alone by train from Munich, Germany, to Milan, Italy, to join his family. Although his parents were glad to see Albert, they were disappointed that he had been expelled from school and worried about what would become of their son.

Albert, however, was delighted to be in Italy. People seemed much more relaxed and friendly there than they did in Germany. He spoke later of his first impressions of the country:

> I was so surprised when I crossed the Alps to Italy to see how the ordinary Italian, the ordinary man and woman, uses words and expressions of a high level of thought and cultural content so different from the ordinary German. This is due to their long cultural history. . . . The people of Northern Italy are the most civilized people I have ever met.[2]

Not long after Albert arrived, he and his father looked for a new school. They knew that without an education, Albert would not find a good job. They settled on the Zurich Polytechnic, a well-known technical college in Zurich, Switzerland. Albert's father liked the school because of its technical training program. Albert

A scene in Milan, Italy, where Einstein rejoined his family at the age of fifteen.

liked it because he wanted to become a teacher and Polytechnic offered a teaching degree. Also, if he passed the entrance exam, he would be accepted without a high school diploma.

Hard Lessons

Albert approached the test with the wrong attitude, however. He did not study the subjects that did not interest him, such as languages and biology. Thus, he did well in the mathematics portion but failed the rest of the entrance exam. He was not allowed to enter the college. But the professors were so impressed by his math scores that they told him they would enroll him without an-

Einstein uses math equations to explain his theories. As a student, he did poorly in many subjects but always did well in math.

other entrance exam if he earned his high school diploma.

To do this, Albert enrolled in high school in Aarau, Switzerland, and he earned his diploma. A year later he was accepted at the Polytechnic in Zurich, and his mother's wealthy family provided him with an allowance to help pay his expenses. Once again, though, Albert allowed his attitude to get in the way of his opportunities. He studied only what interested him, was sarcastic toward his professors, and skipped classes he did not like.

Graduation

By borrowing notes from classmates, he was able to study enough to pass and graduate, but he went no further at the school. Most graduates were offered entry-level teaching positions at the Polytechnic, but Albert was not. His attitude had made him unpopular with many of his professors, and they did not want to work with him.

When Albert graduated from college, he had no job, and the allowance from his mother's family ended. They felt that since he now had an education, he should be able to provide for himself. With no money and no prospects, Albert would have to take whatever kind of job he could find.

Chapter Two

A Time of Discovery

As a young adult needing to make his living for the first time, Albert Einstein made a number of discoveries. One of these discoveries was that jobs could be hard to find.

Opportunities and Conflicts

In May 1901, Einstein found a temporary teaching position in Winterthur, Switzerland, covering for a teacher who was away on military service. This job lasted from May through July. Though brief, it was a good position. Einstein taught several math classes, the subject he most enjoyed teaching. This job also provided him with comfortable living quarters.

Many Sundays during this period Einstein traveled from Winterthur to Zurich by train to see his girlfriend, Mileva Merick, whom he had met at Polytechnic. It was a happy time, but because he did not have a permanent job, he could not afford to marry her.

When the regular math teacher returned, Einstein had to search for other work. He found a position in

Einstein leans against shelves of scientific books and papers at his home in Berlin, Germany, in the 1920s.

Schaffhausen, also in Switzerland, tutoring two male high school students in mathematics. For his services he received a room, meals, and a small salary.

The job barely supported him, though, and he and the boys' father had many differences of opinion over how math should be taught. But because it was the only job he could find at the time, Einstein tried to make it work. He wrote to his school friend, Marcel Grossman: "Although such a position is not ideal for an independent nature. . . . I believe it will leave me some time for my favorite studies so that at least I shall not become rusty."[3]

But after just four months on this job, he was fired. The boys' father thought Einstein was too informal with the boys and did not like his attitude. Once again Einstein was out of a job and no closer to marrying Mileva.

He advertised in the newspaper as a private tutor but made very little money. Finally he received a message that raised his spirits, a message that would provide solutions to many of his problems.

The Patent Office

In 1902 Einstein's school friend, Marcel Grossman, learned of a job in the **patent** office in Berne, Switzerland, and he recommended Einstein for the position. A patent is a document that gives the inventor of a device ownership of that device. Other people cannot make or sell the device without the permission of the patent holder. Einstein was desperate for work and glad to have any full-time job, even if it was not teaching.

Berne, Switzerland, where Einstein worked in a patent office in 1902.

Einstein was happy to be selected for the patent office job for several reasons. First, he was out of money. Second, the thought of working with patents for inventions appealed to his curious nature. And third he finally made enough money to support a wife. Einstein married Mileva Merick on January 6, 1903. Another happy event that occurred during Einstein's years at the patent office was the birth of his first son, Hans Albert, on May 14, 1904. A second son, Eduard, was born in July 1909. In later years Einstein spoke of his time at the patent office as being some of the happiest and most productive years of his life.

Early Theories

It was during the patent office years that Einstein published several research papers in an important German science journal, *Annals of Physics*. One paper was on the theory of special relativity. Special relativity is an explanation about motion. Einstein said the speed of an object depends on the point from which the object in motion is being watched. Another paper was on the photoelectric effect. In this theory Einstein said that light, under certain conditions, moves as a stream of particles called **photons**. The photoelectric effect led to the development of many inventions, including television and lasers. Finally, Einstein published a paper about mass and energy. The ideas explained in this paper led to the development of the atomic bomb.

Einstein hoped his papers would quickly gain the notice of the scientific community, but attention did not come until 1906. That year Max Planck, a famous German physicist, wrote Einstein a letter questioning the theory of special relativity. Because a scientist of Planck's reputation showed an interest in Einstein's theory, other scientists began taking notice of the young scientist and his theories. Einstein's fame grew steadily. He proposed new ways of thinking at a time when scientists were looking for new frontiers for research. They were ready to listen to his ideas.

Einstein the Teacher

While scientists in Germany and other countries studied Einstein's theories, Einstein made some career changes. First, he accepted a post at the University of Berne as an apprentice lecturer, someone who is training to be a full-time lecturer. This was a part-time, unpaid position, but Einstein truly wanted to teach mathematics, and this was an opportunity to do that. While he worked as an apprentice lecturer, Einstein also had to keep his job at the patent office to support himself and his family.

Finally, Einstein was offered what he really wanted: a paying position as a teacher. In 1909 Einstein resigned from the patent office in Berne and began a full-time teaching position at the University of Zurich.

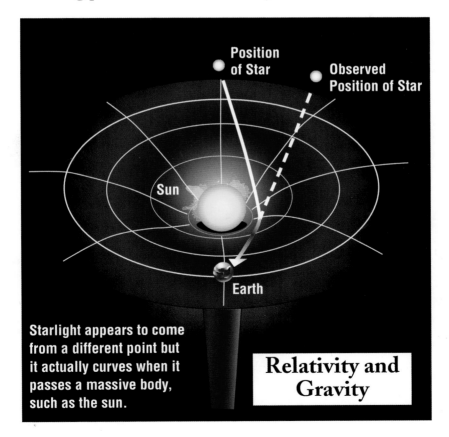

Starlight appears to come from a different point but it actually curves when it passes a massive body, such as the sun.

Relativity and Gravity

A Popular Teacher

In Zurich, Einstein worked long days. He taught six to eight classes per week, and preparing for his classes took several hours. He also spent a lot of his spare time with his students. He met with them after classes at restaurants to discuss his theories and often brought students and other teachers home with him for dinner.

Einstein (left) relaxes with friends in Palm Springs, California, in 1933.

Mileva loved the city of Zurich, but she did not like that her husband spent so much of his time with students and teachers instead of with his family. She was also very busy herself. In early 1909, she was expecting their second child, caring for Hans Albert, and keeping house, in addition to entertaining Einstein's students and colleagues.

More Moves

The family did not stay in Zurich for long. In 1911 Einstein accepted a professorship at the University of Prague, then a part of the Austrian Empire. He received a large salary and could afford a maid to help Mileva with the housekeeping. But Einstein and his wife soon discovered they did not like Prague. In this city there was growing prejudice against Jewish people. A radical political group called the **Nazis** was becoming popular, and the Nazis hated Jews. After eighteen months in Prague, the Einstein family moved back to Zurich, where Einstein accepted a new teaching position. The new job was as a professor at the Polytechnic, the school that had first rejected him as a student and then as a teacher.

Although the Einsteins were happy to be back in Zurich, their stay would not be a long one. After just a few months, Einstein was offered a position at the University of Berlin. This position would allow him more time for research. Without consulting his wife, he accepted the job. Einstein's marriage was already strained, and this decision placed it in even greater jeopardy.

Chapter Three

Success and Changes

By his early thirties, Einstein was a popular teacher. He had acquired a lot of attention with his theory of special relativity and other work. His professional life was gaining success, but his family life was suffering.

Gaining Fame and Growing Apart

As Einstein became more absorbed in his work, he had less time for his family. He was also becoming more famous in the scientific world. He attended meetings with the top scientific minds of the day. And at thirty-one, Einstein was one of the youngest members at a meeting of Europe's top physicists, held in Brussels, Belgium.

The University of Berlin job offer came in 1913. Mileva really did not want to go to Berlin, but in an effort to keep the family together, she and the children made the move with Einstein in the spring of 1914. They did not stay long. Conflicts with her mother-in-law, who had moved to Berlin, and her genuine dislike of the city, was soon more than she could bear. Einstein wrote to a friend: "My wife howls unceasingly about Berlin and her

Einstein receives the model of the medical college building named after him from New York state attorney general Nathaniel Goldstein.

fear of my relatives. . . . My mother is of good disposition, on the whole, but a true devil as a mother-in-law. When she is with us everything is filled with dynamite."[4] By summer, Mileva had returned to Zurich with her sons.

Although Einstein knew his wife was unhappy, her leaving and taking the children with her was a stunning blow. Even though he had little time to spend with his sons, he adored them and missed them terribly. Once they left, he sent most of the family's furniture for their Zurich apartment, sent money for their support, and visited them when he could. Most of Europe was fighting in World War I at the time, though, and travel was difficult. So Einstein rarely saw his sons.

Overwork and Exhaustion

To cope with his loss, Einstein threw himself into his work. While teaching classes and writing, he worked day and night. As a result, in 1917 Einstein had a complete physical and mental collapse. He lost nearly fifty pounds and suffered from ulcers, jaundice, wartime food shortages, and overwork.

Einstein's cousin Elsa, however, also lived in Berlin. When she saw what had happened to her relative, she took it upon herself to nurse him back to health. She saw that he ate properly and got plenty of rest. Elsa's help was fuel for gossip, though. She was a divorced mother of two daughters, and spending so much time in Einstein's apartment placed her reputation in jeopardy. But Einstein and Elsa intended to put the gossip to rest.

By the time of Einstein's collapse, he and his wife had lived apart for nearly three years. He had asked Mileva for a divorce prior to his illness. Now he insisted on it.

A Family Again

Between 1917 and 1919, thanks in great part to Elsa's nursing, Einstein's health slowly recovered. He was divorced from Mileva in February 1919, and he married Elsa the following June. (In Germany, it was acceptable for cousins to marry.) Einstein also adopted Elsa's two daughters, Margot and Ilse, and was happy to be part of

Einstein delivers a lecture in Washington, D.C., in 1940. The famous physicist worked hard throughout his life.

a family again. Unlike Mileva, Elsa got along well with Einstein's mother, who moved in with them briefly in 1920, shortly before her death from cancer.

Although Einstein loved his new family, he was still obsessed with his work. He sometimes became so involved in his studies that he paid little attention to what he was doing. For example, his stepdaughter Margot once became worried because Einstein had been in the

Albert Einstein, his second wife, Elsa (center), and Elsa's daughter Margot pose for a portrait in their Berlin, Germany, home in 1929.

bathroom for a very long time. Concerned for his safety, she called to him through the door. Einstein quickly answered and told her he had been soaking in the bathtub, thinking about a scientific problem. He had become so absorbed with his thoughts that he forgot he was in the bathtub. Another time, his wife had to remind him to put on his underwear.

Turbulent Times

Einstein's home was a peaceful haven, but the city of Berlin was not. Even though Einstein was one of the most respected scientists of the day, the fact that he was Jewish brought his work under attack.

The Nazis started to harass him. Einstein began receiving threatening letters, and some of his lectures were booed by people who supported the Nazis. In addition, Einstein was a **pacifist**, a person totally opposed to war, and was against Germany being at war. This only increased the Nazis' hatred of him. So when Einstein saw the opportunity to take his family away from Berlin, he did.

A Man on the Move

In January 1921 the Russian-born chemist Chaim Weitzmann invited Einstein to travel with him to the United States to help raise money to start a Hebrew university in Jerusalem. Many Jewish people were going to Jerusalem to escape the persecution of some European countries, and Weitzmann felt Jerusalem needed a university so that young Jewish people could be educated.

Einstein was interested in the plans for a Hebrew university, so he agreed to go to America.

The Einsteins and Weitzmann arrived in New York City on April 11, 1921. Einstein won over the American press and the American people right away. His humor and charm made a very favorable impression. And Einstein's popularity helped raise pledges of almost $4 million for the university in Jerusalem.

Einstein laughs out loud during a lunch in 1953. The public always found him to be funny and charming.

A Dangerous Position

The trip to America was only the beginning of Einstein's travels. He returned briefly to Germany, then continued on to Switzerland, France, and Japan, where he spoke to scientific groups. On October 8, 1922, while on a trip to Japan, Einstein learned that he had been awarded the 1921 Nobel Prize in **physics** for his work on the photo-electric effect, a study that had begun with a paper originally published in 1905. Because the Einsteins were aboard ship and the news caught them by surprise, their celebration was a modest one.

Although they kept their apartment in Berlin for more than ten years, the Einsteins were rarely home. Einstein was in constant demand as a lecturer, and this kept him traveling much of the time. Because the Nazis were gaining popularity and control in Germany, he took his family with him to make sure they were safe. By the early 1930s, conditions in Berlin were so dangerous that Einstein knew he and his family would have to make a permanent move.

Chapter Four

A New Home and a Different World

As the decade of the 1930s began, the Nazis were gaining more attention and greater power. **Anti-Semitism**, prejudice against Jews, was on the rise in Germany. Jewish people lost their jobs and the Nazis took away their property. Despite his fame, Einstein, too, was victimized by Nazis.

Persecution and a New Home

In January 1933, Adolf Hitler was appointed the leader of Germany. By February he had assumed the powers of a dictator. This meant he was in total control of that country. He was also the leader of the Nazis, so Jews such as Albert Einstein found themselves in a lot of trouble.

In 1933, while away from Germany on one of his trips, Einstein received word that the Nazis had broken into his Berlin apartment and his summer home, and taken all the money from his Berlin bank account. He also heard that the Nazis had offered $5,000 to anyone who would kill him. "I didn't know I was worth that much!"[5] Einstein joked.

Even though he tried to stay lighthearted, Einstein knew that his situation was serious. His friend Paul Schwartz voiced concern. "If you go to Germany, Albert, they will drag you through the streets by the hair."[6]

Einstein knew that he and his family could not return to Germany as long as Hitler was in power. He also believed they would be safer outside of Europe. So, he accepted a teaching position at Princeton University in Princeton, New Jersey. He began work in the fall of 1933.

New Beginnings

The Einsteins moved to Princeton in October 1933. They settled into their new home, a few short blocks from where Einstein would teach his classes, and hoped for the privacy and safety they had not had in Berlin.

Relatives surround Einstein (third from right) in 1930 just before he leaves Berlin to go to the United States.

Einstein enjoyed his new home in Princeton, New Jersey, and became popular with his neighbors.

The Einsteins' neighbors were proud to have such a famous person in their community and did what they could to protect the family's privacy. For example, they turned down requests for interviews by nosy reporters.

Princeton neighbors soon got used to seeing the frizzy-haired, sockless Einstein in his wrinkled clothes and scuffed shoes, walking to and from the campus. He never learned to drive a car, so he walked most days. In the cold months someone drove him to and from work.

The fun-loving Einstein quickly became a favorite of neighborhood children. When they asked him why he wore no socks, he told them that he was so old he did not have to wear them. He also had a special talent that increased his popularity: He could wiggle his ears.

Tragic Loss

Einstein and Elsa were happy in their new home. Margot and Ilse, both grown, were also safely out of Germany and living in France. The family's happiness, however, was short-lived. Ilse had a disease called **tuberculosis** and soon became seriously ill. Elsa traveled to Paris to care for her daughter, but there was nothing she could do. Ilse died in 1934.

Elsa returned to Princeton with Margot, but tragedy soon struck again. Elsa's own health began to fail. She suffered from heart disease and a kidney disorder. After a long illness, Elsa died on December 21, 1936.

For a while, just Einstein and Margot occupied the Mercer Street house in Princeton. In 1939, though, Einstein's sister Maja, by then widowed, came from Europe to live with them. Her move was timely because Germany invaded Poland a few months later and Europe plunged into World War II.

War and the Atomic Age

By 1939 Einstein and many other people were very concerned about how much power the Nazis had. In July of

Einstein (center), his secretary, Helene Dukas (left), and his daughter Margot, are sworn in as U.S. citizens in New Jersey in 1940.

that year, scientists Otto Hahn and Lise Meitner visited Einstein at Princeton to share their worries with him. They were concerned that Germany might produce an atomic bomb, a weapon more powerful than any they had seen before.

After the meeting, Einstein wrote a letter to President Franklin D. Roosevelt. He urged the president to have U.S. scientists go to work right away to develop the bomb themselves. In fact, when America did develop the bomb a few years later, scientists used Einstein's own theories to do it. Because of this, Einstein was called the Father of the Atomic Bomb. But he did not like this title because he was still a pacifist at heart.

Despite this, Einstein threw his support behind his adopted country. He and Margot became U.S. citizens on October 1, 1940, and they voted in their first presidential election a month later. He also worked to raise money for the war effort.

Bombings in Japan

Einstein hoped until the last moment that the atomic bomb would not have to be used, but his hope did not come true. One bomb was dropped on Hiroshima, Japan, on August 6, 1945. Three days later, another bomb was dropped on Nagasaki, Japan. Japan had sided with Germany during the war and had attacked the United States at Pearl Harbor, Hawaii, three and a half years earlier. The bombing of Hiroshima and Nagasaki brought the war to an end.

By that time, Einstein was very old, but he was as popular as ever. He was offered the presidency of Israel in 1952, but turned it down because of his age, his failing health, and his lack of political experience.

A Quiet Ending

Throughout his life, Einstein believed that scientists should be known for their ideas, not their popularity. And this belief was evident in one of his final requests.

Einstein in the early 1950s. His theories are still discussed and pondered today.

Before his death in 1955, Einstein asked that his body be cremated and his ashes scattered in a place the press and the public did not know about. He also asked that his home remain a home. He did not want it turned into a museum or a shrine. In this way, Einstein ensured that his neighbors, who had been so loyal to him, would not be bothered by tourists. His final wishes were honored.

Notes

Chapter 1: Differences and Difficulties

1. Quoted in Michael White and John Gribbin, *Einstein: A Life in Science*. New York: Penguin Books, 1994, p. 5.
2. Quoted in Albrecht Folsing, *Albert Einstein*. New York: Penguin Books, 1997, p. 34.

Chapter 2: A Time of Discovery

3. Quoted in Denis Brian, *Einstein: A Life*. New York: John Wiley & Sons, 1997, p. 39.

Chapter 3: Success and Changes

4. Quoted in Brian, *Einstein*, p. 87.

Chapter 4: A New Home and a Different World

5. Quoted in Brian, *Einstein*, p. 249.
6. Quoted in Brian, *Einstein*, p. 244.

Glossary

anti-Semitism: Prejudice against people of Jewish heritage or the Jewish religion.

Nazis: A radical political group that controlled Germany from 1933 to 1945. Led by Adolf Hitler, this group was responsible for killing millions of Jewish people during World War II.

pacifist: A person who is opposed to war.

patent: A document that makes it illegal for any other person to create and sell a product without the permission of the person who invented or developed the product.

photons: Particles of light energy.

physics: The study of and the relationship between matter and energy.

theory: A scientific idea proposed to explain something.

tuberculosis: A disease caused by bacteria that affects the intestines, the respiratory system, and can also attack the bloodstream.

For Further Exploration

Joyce Goldenstern, *Albert Einstein: Physicist and Genius.* Springfield, NJ: Enslow Publishers, 1995. Biography of the famous scientist with black-and-white photographs and suggested activities for children.

Fiona McDonald, *Albert Einstein: Genius Behind the Theory of Relativity.* Woodbridge, CT: Blackbirch Press, 2000. A biography of the scientist who changed the way we look at space and time. Contains middle-grade to junior-high-school vocabulary.

Stephanie McPherson, *Ordinary Genius: The Story of Albert Einstein.* Minneapolis: Carolrhoda Books, 1995. A comprehensive middle-grade biography of the famous physicist.

John B. Severance, *Einstein: Visionary Scientist.* New York: Clarion Books, 1999. A biography of the great scientist, with excellent black-and-white photographs and a comprehensive chronology.

Index

Picture Credits

About the Author

Sheila Wyborny is a retired science and social studies teacher living in Houston, Texas, with her husband of more than thirty years. She likes to read in her spare time, and she and her husband enjoy taking trips in their airplane, named Lucy.